PIPER
THE
POLAR
BEAR

JENNY SCHREIBER

Piper the Polar Bear

Jenny Schreiber
Star Valley, WY 83110

In Association with
Elite Online Publishing
63 East 11400 South #230
Sandy, UT 84070
EliteOnlinePublishing.com

ISBN: 978-1513677026 (Paperback)

ISBN: 978-1513677149 (Hardback)

PIPER
THE
POLAR
BEAR

JENNY SCHREIBER

Meet Piper.
Piper is a
Polar Bear.

Piper is an
Ice Bear.

The polar bear
is known as the
"white bear".

She Lives in the Arctic Circle which is the northern most part of the earth.

Piper was born on land, but she spends most of her time on the sea ice and in the water.

Piper eats meat.

She hunts
for seals.

Piper can smell the seal up to one mile away, and buried under three feet of snow.

Piper likes to sleep. She sleeps like a human, about 7-8 hours per day.

She is one of
the largest bear
species.

Piper can weigh
up to 350–700 kg
(770–1,500 lbs.)

Piper likes the
cold weather.

She moves across the snow, ice, and open water.

Sometimes she travels up to 1,100 Miles (1,800 Kilometers).

Piper is an excellent swimmer and often will swim for days.

When she has a family she has one or two bear cubs. The babies live with her until they are 2-3 years old.

She can live
to about
25 years old.

Polar Bears live in
Canada,
Greenland,
Norway,
Russia, and
the United States.

The End

Find More books by Jenny Schreiber

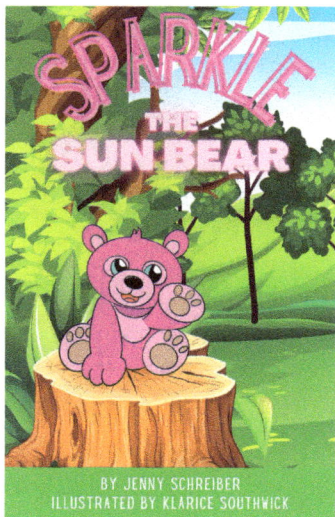

Sparkle the Sun Bear

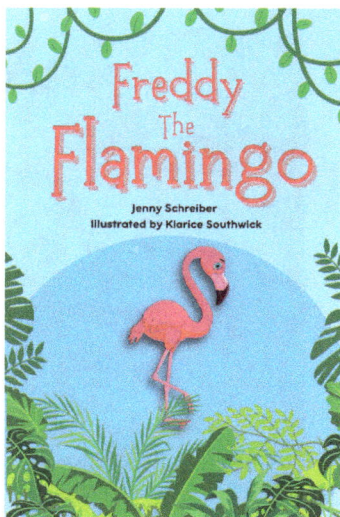

Freddy the Flamingo

Piper the
Polar Bear

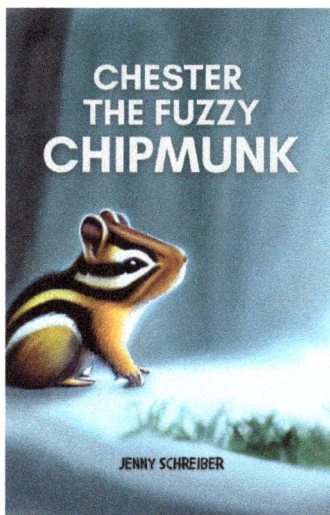

Chester the
Fuzzy Chipmunk

Animal Facts Children's Book Series

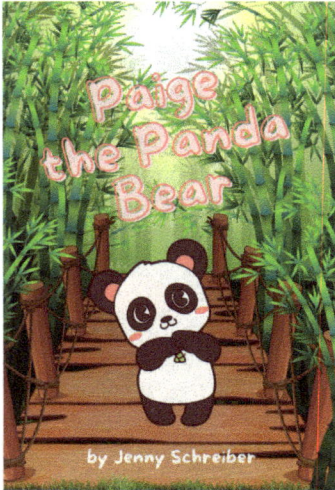

Paige the
Panda Bear

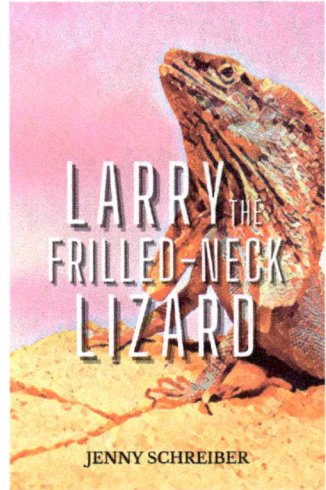

Larry the
Frilled-Neck Lizard

www.ingramcontent.com/pod-product-compliance
Lightning Source LLC
Chambersburg PA
CBHW071823050426
42335CB00063BA/1786